Cephalopods

Sally Cowan

Cephalopods

Text: Sally Cowan
Publishers: Tania Mazzeo and Eliza Webb
Series consultant: Amanda Sutera
  Hands on Heads Consulting
Editor: Sarah Layton
Project editor: Annabel Smith
Designer: Leigh Ashforth
Project designer: Danielle Maccarone
Diagrams: David Rojas Marquez
Permissions researcher: Helen Mammides
Production controller: Renee Tome

Acknowledgements
We would like to thank the following for permission to reproduce
copyright material:

Front cover: Alamy Stock Photo/Blue Planet Archive; pp. 1, 31 (top):
Nature Picture Library/Joel Sartore/Photo Ark; p. 4 (left): Alamy Stock
Photo/Juniors Bildarchiv GmbH, (right): Alamy Stock Photo/Jeff Rotman;
p. 5 (left): Alamy Stock Photo/imageBROKER.com GmbH & Co. KG, (right):
iStock.com/peilien; p. 6: Getty Images/Reinhard Dirscherl; p. 8: iStock.
com/Bao Le; p. 9: Alamy Stock Photo/Jeff Rotman; pp. 11, 30 (left): iStock.
com/TheSP4N1SH; p. 12: Alamy Stock Photo/Underwater Imaging;
p. 13 (main): Alamy Stock Photo/BIOSPHOTO, (inset): iStock.com/Suljo;
p. 14 (main): iStock.com/Alexey Masliy, (inset): iStock.com/THIERRY
EIDENWEIL; p. 15 (top): iStock.com/Brian Scantlebury, (centre): Alamy
Stock Photo/Brandon Cole Marine Photography, (bottom): Alamy Stock
Photo/Georgette Apol; p. 16 (main): Shutterstock.com/SergeUWPhoto,
(inset): Science Source/Dante Fenolio; p. 17 (main): AAP Images/Professor
Peter Godfrey Smith, (inset): Alamy Stock Photo/Minden Pictures;
p. 18: Science Photo Library/LOUISE MURRAY; p. 19: iStock.com/Michael
Stubblefield; p. 20: Oceanwide Images/© Gary Bell; p. 21 (main): Alamy
Stock Photo/Blue Planet Archive, (inset): iStock.com/David_Slater;
p. 22: Alamy Stock Photo/Carlos Villoch - MagicSea.com; p. 23 (main):
Alamy Stock Photo/Moodboard Stock Photography, (inset): iStock.com/
JianGang Wang; p. 24 (main): Shutterstock.com/Rich Carey, (inset):
Shutterstock.com/Gerry Bishop; p. 25: iStock.com/Placebo365; p. 26
(top left), back cover: Alamy Stock Photo/Wildestanimal; p. 26 (main):
Alamy Stock Photo/Reinhard Dirscherl; p. 27: Shutterstock.com/elena
moiseeva; p. 28: Alamy Stock Photo/imageBROKER.com GmbH & Co. KG;
p. 29: Science Source/Douglas Faulkner; p. 30 (right): Shutterstock.com/
NaturePicsFilms; p. 31 (bottom left): Shutterstock.com/David A Litman,
(bottom right): Shutterstock.com/Wildestanimal.

Every effort has been made to trace and acknowledge copyright.
However, if any infringement has occurred, the publishers tender their
apologies and invite the copyright holders to contact them.

NovaStar

Text © 2024 Cengage Learning Australia Pty Limited
Illustrations © 2024 Cengage Learning Australia Pty Limited

ISBN 978 0 17 033439 6

Cengage Learning Australia
Level 5, 80 Dorcas Street
Southbank VIC 3006 Australia
Phone: 1300 790 853
Email: aust.nelsonprimary@cengage.com

For learning solutions, visit cengage.com.au

Printed in China by 1010 Printing International Ltd
1 2 3 4 5 6 7 28 27 26 25 24

*Nelson acknowledges the Traditional Owners and Custodians
of the lands of all First Nations Peoples. We pay respect
to Elders past and present, and extend that respect to
all First Nations Peoples today.*

Contents

What Are Cephalopods?

Cephalopods (say: *se-fa-luh-pods*) are a type of animal that lives in the sea. They spend their lives underwater, breathing through their **gills**. But they are not fish. Cephalopods are part of the **mollusc** family. They have soft bodies and no backbones.

There are four groups of cephalopods:

- octopuses
- squids
- cuttlefish
- nautiluses.

a Caribbean reef squid

a common octopus

All cephalopods have an unusual feature: they have at least eight arms. The arms of most cephalopods are covered in hundreds of suckers. Suckers are shaped like small cups and are made of thick muscle. They are used for catching prey and holding onto things when moving around.

Squids and cuttlefish also have tentacles. These have suckers or sharp hooks on the ends. The tentacles are longer than the arms and can shoot out quickly to catch prey.

Cephalopods are clever creatures. Many use camouflage to hide. Some put on amazing colour displays, and others can even light up their bodies.

a chambered nautilus

a broadclub cuttlefish

The Strange Bodies of Cephalopods

The word "cephalopod" means "head-foot" in Greek, and this is a good description of the strange body shape of these animals. A cephalopod's arms are joined to its head. Behind the head is a bag-like body part called the "mantle". It holds the animal's **organs**.

Nautiluses are a bit different. They have an outer shell that protects their soft body.

Nautiluses can stretch their arms out of their protective shell or pull them back in.

The arms and tentacles of cephalopods spread out in a ring around their mouth. This makes it easy for cephalopods to grab prey and bring it straight into their mouth. All cephalopods are **carnivores**. They eat foods like crabs, prawns, fish and shellfish. They have a sharp beak just inside their mouth for cracking shells and bones. The radula is also inside the mouth. This is like a tongue that is lined with sharp teeth for ripping up food.

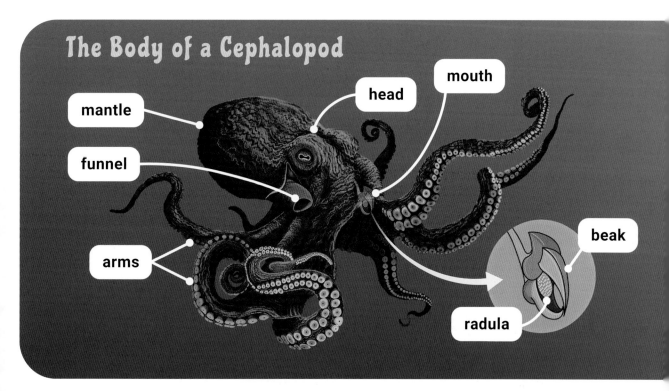

The Body of a Cephalopod

mouth

head

mantle

funnel

beak

arms

radula

Did You Know?

In the past, people believed cephalopods' arms were actually legs. Today, most scientists refer to them as arms.

Cephalopods have two large eyes. They see well in the water, which is useful when searching for prey. But scientists think that cephalopods might not be able to see colours. Instead of seeing colours, their eyes can **detect** changes in light in their underwater habitat.

All cephalopods have a small tube in their bodies called a "funnel". This is found near where the arms join the head. Cephalopods can shoot water out of their funnels and move surprisingly fast in the opposite direction. This way of moving is called jet propulsion.

Cuttlefish can react quickly to very small changes in light.

funnel

Cephalopods move in special ways. Octopuses can hold their arms in tightly as they shoot through the water, or they can move their arms around to change direction. Squids and cuttlefish also have fins, which they flap when they swim. They use their fins to steer and change direction, or to hover in one place.

Squids are the fastest of the cephalopods.

fin

Enormous Eyeballs

The colossal squid has the largest eyes of any living creature. Each eye is about the size of a soccer ball!

Cephalopods have three hearts. One heart pumps blood around the body, while the other two hearts pump blood to the gills. Cephalopod blood is blue! The blue colour is caused by a **mineral** in their blood called copper. Copper is good for moving oxygen around the animal's body in cool water and in deep oceans, where there is not much oxygen in the water.

A Cephalopod's Hearts

three hearts

Red-Blooded Bodies

Humans have a mineral in their blood called iron. This gives our blood its red colour.

All cephalopods have large brains for their body size, but their brains are very different from human brains. Cephalopods have a small central brain and many other brain cells spread throughout their bodies, in their eyes and arms. For example, an octopus's arms can expertly feel their way in different directions at the same time. Though each arm can act for itself, the arms can also suddenly move together for jet propulsion or to help the octopus jump on prey.

Studies show that cephalopods are about as clever as dogs!

A common octopus uses its arms to swim.

Camouflage and Ink

Octopuses, squids and cuttlefish have two other unusual features. They can camouflage themselves and squirt ink from their bodies.

Cephalopods spend their lives being hunted by other sea animals, so camouflage is important for survival. Most cephalopods can change the colour of their skin instantly to blend in with their environment. Their skin is covered in tiny **sacs**, or cells, that hold **pigments** that they can change by moving muscles.

A broadclub cuttlefish blends into a coral reef.

The muscles used for changing colour are controlled by the brain. So, when a cephalopod needs to hide from a predator, communicate with other cephalopods or attract a mate, its brain sends a signal to its skin. Then, the most suitable colours appear on its skin.

Can you spot the Mediterranean octopus hiding here?

Most octopuses, squids and cuttlefish also have ink sacs in their bodies. They can squirt ink into the water whenever they are in danger of attack. The ink spreads in the water and creates a kind of **smokescreen** to help the cephalopod escape from its predator.

An octopus escapes from danger by squirting a cloud of ink behind it.

Octopuses

There are about 300 different **species** of octopus. They live in shallow seas and deep oceans. Octopuses vary in size, from the tiny poisonous blue-ringed octopus to the giant Pacific octopus. The giant Pacific octopus is the largest octopus and can grow up to 9 metres wide, from the tip of one arm to another. New species of octopus are still being discovered.

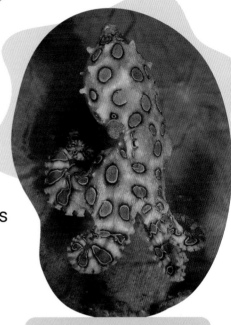

a blue-ringed octopus

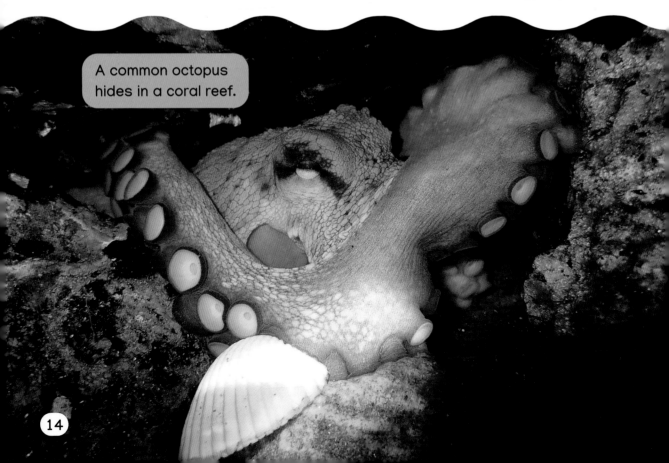

A common octopus hides in a coral reef.

Octopuses have flexible bodies with no hard bone inside. They can squeeze into tight spaces in rocks and coral reefs. This is useful when waiting for prey and hiding from predators, such as sharks and dolphins.

veined octopus

As well as using camouflage, octopuses sometimes disguise themselves as other sea animals to scare off predators. For example, the **mimic** octopus can hide six of its arms in the sand on the sea floor, with the other two arms stretched out to look like a poisonous sea snake. It can also flatten its body to look like a fish swimming along the sea floor.

A mimic octopus hides on the sea floor.

Sandy Snacks

Some octopuses can survive out of water for a short time. They search for prey in rock pools, using their suckers to move.

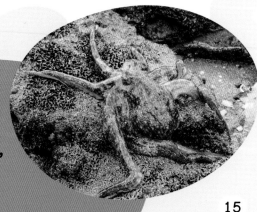

15

Octopuses spend most of their time searching for food. They use their arms or beaks to pull apart clam and mussel shells, as well as crabs and other shellfish. After they eat the creature's insides, they sometimes pick up the empty shells and use them for shelter and protection.

The small flapjack octopus can't grab with its arms, so it uses its beak to hunt.

A coconut octopus pulls together two halves of an empty shell to hide inside.

Twist the Top

Scientists have observed that some octopuses can even open jars!

Scientists thought that octopuses mostly lived alone. But a species called the gloomy octopus has been found living in groups near Sydney, Australia. At two sites, these groups of octopuses have built **dens** very close to each other, using the remains of shells from creatures they have eaten.

A gloomy octopus lives in a den of shells.

Most octopuses only live for about two years. The males die soon after mating. The females lay eggs, then guard them and keep them safe until they hatch. After they hatch, the baby octopuses drift away, and the female usually dies.

Giant Pacific octopus eggs hatch in the ocean.

Squids

About 300 species of squids live in shallow seas and deep oceans. Most squids are shorter than 60 centimetres long. But there are some huge species: the Humboldt squid is about 2 metres long, and the giant squid can be up to 13 metres long. The colossal squid has the longest body of all the squids. Its mantle alone grows to at least 5 metres long.

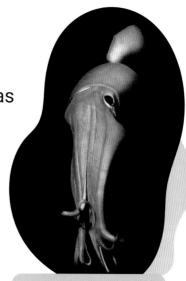

a Humboldt squid

Squids have a tube-shaped body with a hard, straight **structure** inside them called a "pen". Their eight arms are thin and whip-like. They also have two longer tentacles for catching prey. Squids have fins at the top of their mantle.

The Parts of a Squid

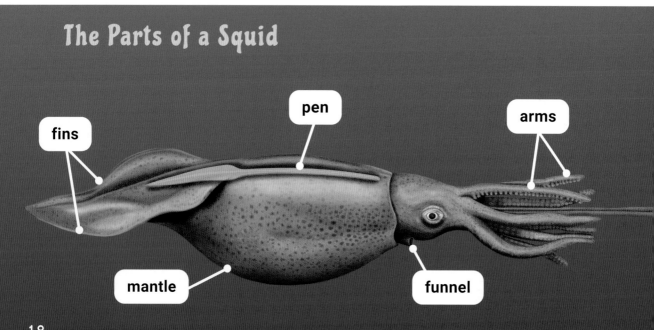

fins

pen

arms

mantle

funnel

Most squids live alone, including the giant squid and the colossal squid. But Humboldt squids sometimes live in shoals, or groups, of more than one thousand. Smaller squids can live in large shoals of more than a million.

A shoal of Caribbean reef squids swim together.

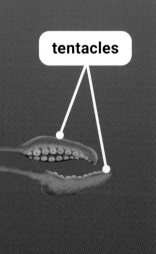

tentacles

A Squid Squad

A group of squids is usually called a shoal, but a few years ago some scientists started a petition to change the name to a squad – a squid squad!

A young bigfin reef squid lights up while swimming at night.

Some squids can light up their bodies. In the dark, deep sea, they use this light to find other squids and send signals to each other. Scientists think that Humboldt squids display flickering lights to avoid bumping into each other when they hunt together. Squids also put on colourful light shows to attract mates.

Down in the Dark

Sunlight cannot reach very deep water. The deeper the water, the darker it is.

The tiny Hawaiian bobtail squid lights up its body, even though it lives in shallow water. It lights up the underside of its body to match the light coming from the sky above. If any predators are hunting below, they cannot see the little squid swimming above.

a Hawaiian bobtail squid

Like octopuses, squids usually do not live for more than a few years. They die soon after mating, leaving masses of squid eggs to float in the water before hatching.

Longfin inshore squid eggs float in the ocean.

Cuttlefish

There are more than 120 species of cuttlefish, and most live in warm, shallow waters. Cuttlefish are usually less than 30 centimetres long, except for the giant cuttlefish. It can grow up to one metre long and is the largest kind of cuttlefish.

Cuttlefish have a hard, flat cuttlebone inside their bodies. A cuttlebone is similar to shell, but with tiny holes in it that can hold water. The more water there is in the cuttlebone, the heavier the cuttlefish's body is. It can sink to the sea floor and stay there. When there is less water in the cuttlebone, the cuttlefish rises in the water.

A cuttlefish uses its funnel to propel itself.

The Parts of a Cuttlefish

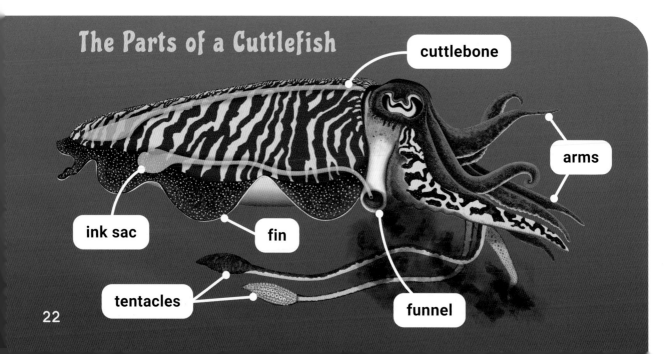

cuttlebone

arms

ink sac

fin

tentacles

funnel

A cuttlefish moves gracefully through the ocean by flapping its fins.

Like squids, cuttlefish have eight arms and two longer tentacles, which they use to catch prey such as fish, crabs and prawns. They also eat smaller cuttlefish.

As well as moving by jet propulsion, cuttlefish can move more slowly by flapping the two large, wavy fins that extend along the sides of their body.

Cooking with Ink

For hundreds of years, cuttlefish ink was used in pens for writing. Today, people use cuttlefish ink in cooking to add a salty flavour and dark colour to foods like pasta.

Cuttlefish have unusual eyes with W-shaped **pupils**. Their eyes are the most **sensitive** of all the cephalopods. Cuttlefish can change colour instantly when the light in their habitat changes. Some can also change their shape to trick predators. The small pharaoh cuttlefish can change its shape to look like a hermit crab.

Up close, a cuttlefish's pupil looks like the letter W.

A cuttlefish can quickly make itself more or less visible.

A male cuttlefish (right) changes its patterns to look like a female cuttlefish.

Cuttlefish communicate by displaying different patterns on their skin. They put on spectacular displays to attract mates. Hundreds of cuttlefish can gather in one place when it is time to find a mate. The males sometimes fight each other, but the smaller male cuttlefish have a clever trick for avoiding attack. They display female patterns on their skin so they can swim past the large males unharmed. Then the little males can safely move closer to the females to mate.

Most cuttlefish only live for a year or two. They die soon after mating.

Nautiluses

There are only 11 species of nautiluses. They mostly live in tropical parts of the western Pacific Ocean. They are different from the other cephalopods because they have an outer shell covering their soft bodies, and more than 90 arms.

A nautilus shell is a coiled shape, like a wound-up circle, and is usually white with brown stripes. The stripes provide camouflage as the nautilus moves through its watery habitat.

Nautiluses can tuck their arms into their shells.

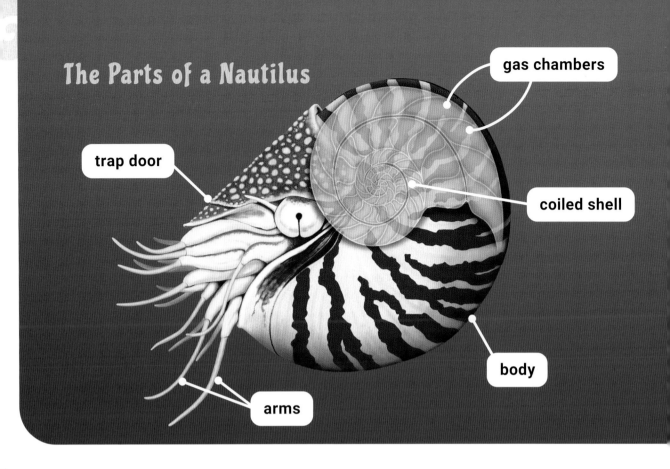

The Parts of a Nautilus

gas chambers

trap door

coiled shell

body

arms

Nautiluses have a spotted, leathery trap door that can close over their arms. The shell can give them some protection from predators. But nautiluses can still be eaten by sharks and any other fish or turtle with teeth that are strong enough to break their shell. They are even eaten by octopuses.

Splendid Shells

A major threat to the survival of nautiluses is people, who often collect these animals for their beautiful shells.

Nautiluses can move up and down in the sea by changing the amounts of water and gas in small **chambers** inside their shells. The nautiluses move by nodding backwards and forwards while floating or sinking through the water. They can also move fast using jet propulsion.

A chambered nautilus swims through the water.

Each day, these animals rest on the sea floor or on reefs. Then, at night, they rise to shallow waters to find food. The eyes of nautiluses are not as sensitive as those of other cephalopods. They probably do not see very well, so they rely on their sense of smell to find food. They eat shellfish and also feed on dead animals. Nautilus arms have sticky grooves for catching food.

Nautiluses can live for 20 years, which is the longest lifespan of all the cephalopods. They can mate more than once, but not until the females are about 10 years old.

A nautilus feeds on the ocean floor.

The Same and Different

Cephalopods are an unusual group of animals.
With their strange bodies and clever brains,
they are some of the world's most interesting animals.

Octopuses	Squids
• have eight arms • have a soft body with no hard bones • can change colour • can change the **texture** of their skin • have an ink sac	• have eight arms and two tentacles • have a tube-shaped body with a long, thin "pen" inside • have fins at the top of their mantle • can change colour • have an ink sac

a common octopus

a reef squid

a giant Pacific octopus

 ## Cuttlefish

 ## Nautiluses

Cuttlefish
- have eight arms and two tentacles
- have a flat cuttlebone inside their body
- have fins along the sides of their body
- can change colour
- have an ink sac

Nautiluses
- have more than 90 arms
- have an outer shell covering their soft bodies
- can't change colour
- do not have an ink sac

a common European cuttlefish

a nautilus

Glossary

carnivores (*noun*)   animals that eat other animals

chambers (*noun*)   spaces inside a body

dens (*noun*)   hidden homes that some wild animals use

detect (*verb*)   to notice something that is not easy to see

gills (*noun*)   small holes in the sides of a sea creature's body that allow it to breathe oxygen

mimic (*verb*)   to copy something

mineral (*noun*)   a non-living material found in nature

mollusc (*noun*)   an animal with a soft body, often protected by an outer shell

organs (*noun*)   parts of the body, like the heart or the brain

pigments (*noun*)   substances that give colour to things

pupils (*noun*)   the small, round black area in the middle of the eye

sacs (*noun*)   bag-like body parts that often contain liquid

sensitive (*adjective*)   quick to react to small changes

smokescreen (*noun*)   a cloud of smoke used to hide

species (*noun*)   different types of plants or animals

structure (*noun*)   an arrangement of parts, a framework

texture (*noun*)   the way things feel and look, either rough or smooth

Index